HO'OPONOPONO

I'M SORRY

PLEASE FORGIVE ME

THANK YOU

I LOVE YOU

By Stephen Cartledge

*YOU WHO ARE A REFLECTION
OF THE THOUGHT
THAT I AM LESS THAN
WHOLE AND PERFECT
I EMBRACE YOU
I TAKE YOU INTO MY HEART
I INTEGRATE WITH YOU
FOR I AM LOVE
AND MY LOVE ENCOMPASSES
ALL THAT SEEMINGLY IS NOT LOVE
I DO NOT FEAR YOU
I DO NOT HOLD YOU AT A DISTANCE
I EMBRACE YOU
I WRAP MY ARMS AROUND YOU
THESE INFINITE ARMS
THAT KNOW THAT ALL YOU ARE
I AM
SO WHEN I LOVE MYSELF
I LOVE YOU
WHEN I LOVE MYSELF
I ACKNOWLEDGE THAT*

I AM WHOLE AND PERFECT
AS PART OF ME
YOU ARE WHOLE AND PERFECT TOO
WHEN I SEE THE SEEMING ERROR
OF YOUR WAYS I WILL
I WILL LOVE MYSELF AND SAY
I AM SO SORRY
PLEASE FORGIVE ME
I LOVE YOU

CONNIE CRANE

A PRAYER OF FORGIVENESS

"If I have harmed anyone in any way either knowingly or unknowingly through my own confusions I ask their forgiveness.

If anyone has harmed me in any way either knowingly or unknowingly through their own confusions I forgive them.

And if there is a situation I am not ready to forgive I forgive myself for that.

For all the ways that I harm myself, negate, doubt, belittle myself, judge or be unkind to myself through my own confusions I forgive myself"

ABOUT THE AUTHOR

Stephen Cartledge was born in September 1958, in Dover, United Kingdom.
When he left school in 1975 he was lost, had no direction the only thing he knew was, he did not want to be tied down in a dead end job here in Sheffield UK.
He decided to travel Europe to find himself, what was his purpose in life. Whilst traveling he was living on the streets, the beaches, where ever he could rest that was him and he was happy, happy and free. One day I was given a book to read by a guy called David . David was just another traveller who entitled his book or should I say journal " To give gratitude to get what you want", WOW! I couldn't believe he had wrote such powerful words.

From that day on I've studied and used manifestation throughout my life and had some amazing results.
In the early 2000's he lost everything, lost his direction and lost being in control.
Move on today, Stephen now lives in his own house built and planed with my Thai wife here in Northern Thailand, The law of Attraction is once again a big part of my life. Now into my 60's I finally got down to write about me, my journey using LOA, and continue my many years of study on Ho'oponopono.
Stephens first book;
" Me, My journey, and the law of attraction"
was written about his passion for travel, manifestation and the law of attraction.
Stephens other passions when not writing are, Photography, travel and music.

CHAPTERS

Chapter 1. History of Ho'oponpono

Chapter 2. Ho'oponopono and the 12 Spiritual laws

chapter 3. Dr. Ihaleakala Hew Len

chapter 4. Practice Ho'oponopono

HO'OPONOPONO

i'm sorry, please forgive me, thank-you, I love you.

What do these words mean?

"I'm sorry" is acknowledgement that I created whatever pain I've cause or mistakes I've made.

"please forgive me" because I didn't know what was inside of me.

"thank-you" for allowing me to cleanse and erase this memory.

" I love you" my inner divinity meaning "I love you".

CHAPTER 1.

Ho'oponopono [ho.ʔo.po.no.po.no] *is a Hawaiian practice of reconciliation and forgiveness. The Hawaiian word translates into English simply as correction, with the synonyms manage or supervise, and the antonym careless. Similar forgiveness practices are performed on islands throughout the South Pacific, including Hawaii, Samoa, Tahiti and New Zealand. Traditional Ho'oponopono is practiced by Indigenous Hawaiian healers, often within the extended family by a family member. There is also a New Age practice that goes by the same name. In many Polynesian cultures, it is believed that a person's errors (called hara or hala) caused illness. Some believe error angers the gods, others that it attracts malevolent gods, and still others believe the guilt caused by error made one sick. "In most cases, however, specific 'untie-error' rites could be performed to atone for such errors and thereby diminish one's accumulation of them.*

Among the islands of Vanuatu in the South Pacific, people believe that illness usually is caused by sexual misconduct or anger. "If you are angry for two or three days, sickness will come," said one local man. The therapy that counters this sickness is confession. The patient, or a family member, may confess. If no one confesses an error, the patient may die. The Vanuatu people believe that secrecy is what gives power to the illness. When the error is confessed, it no longer has power over the person.

Like many other islanders, including Hawaiians, people of Tikopia in the Solomon Islands, and on Rarotonga in the Cook Islands, believe that the sins of the father will fall upon the children. If a child is sick, the parents are suspected of quarreling or misconduct. In addition to sickness, social disorder could cause sterility of land or other disasters. Harmony could be restored only by confession and apology.

In Pukapuka, it was customary to hold sort of a confessional over patients to determine an appropriate course of action in order to heal them.

Similar traditions are found in Samoa, Tahiti, and among the Maori of New Zealand.

Etymology

"Ho'oponopono" is defined in the Hawaiian Dictionary as:

(a) "To put to rights; to put in order or shape, correct, revise, adjust, amend, regulate, arrange, rectify, tidy up make orderly or neat, administer, superintend, supervise, manage, edit, work carefully or neatly; to make ready, as canoemen preparing to catch a wave."

(b) "Mental cleansing: family conferences in which relationships were set right (ho'oponopono) through prayer, discussion, confession, repentance, and mutual restitution and forgiveness."

Literally, hoʻo is a particle used to make an actualizing verb from the following noun. Here, it creates a verb from the noun pono, which is defined as: "...goodness, uprightness, morality, moral qualities, correct or proper procedure, excellence, well-being, prosperity, welfare, benefit, true condition or nature, duty; moral, fitting, proper, righteous, right, upright, just, virtuous, fair, beneficial, successful, in perfect order, accurate, correct, eased, relieved; should, ought, must, necessary."

Ponopono is defined as "to put to rights; to put in order or shape, correct, revise, adjust, amend, regulate, arrange, rectify, tidy up, make orderly or neat."

Traditional practice

Hawaiian scholar Nana Veary in her book, Change We Must: My Spiritual Journey wrote that ho'oponopono was a practice in Ancient Hawaii and this is supported by oral histories from contemporary Hawaiian elders. Pukui first recorded her experiences and observations from her childhood (born 1895) in her 1958 book.

Although the word ho'oponopono was not used, early Hawaiian historians documented a belief that illness was caused by breaking kapu, or spiritual laws, and that the illness could not be cured until the sufferer atoned for this transgression, often with the assistance of a praying priest (kahuna pule) or healing priest (kahuna lapaʻau). Forgiveness was sought from the gods or from the person with whom there was a dispute.

Pukui described it as a practice of extended family members meeting to "make right" broken family relations. Some families met daily or weekly, to prevent problems from erupting. Others met when a person became ill, believing that illness was caused by the stress of anger, guilt, recriminations and lack of forgiveness.

Kupuna Nana Veary wrote that when any of the children in her family fell ill, her grandmother would ask the parents, "What have you done?" They believed that healing could come only with complete forgiveness of the whole family.

Ritual

Ho'oponopono corrects, restores and maintains good relationships among family members and with their gods or God by getting to the causes and sources of trouble. Usually the most senior member of the family conducts it. He or she gathers the family together. If the family is unable to work through a problem, they turn to a respected outsider.

The process begins with prayer. A statement of the problem is made, and the transgression discussed. Family members are expected to work problems through and cooperate, not "hold fast to the fault". One or more periods of silence may be taken for reflection on the entanglement of emotions and injuries. Everyone's feelings are acknowledged. Then confession, repentance and forgiveness take place. Everyone releases (kala) each other, letting go. They cut off the past ('oki), and together they close the event with a ceremonial feast, called pani, which often included eating limu kala or kala seaweed, symbolic of the release.

In a form used by the family of kahuna Makaweliweli of the island of Moloka'i, the completion of ho'oponopono is represented by giving the person forgiven a lei made from the fruit of the hala tree.

Traditional applications
In the late 20th century, courts in Hawai'i began to order juvenile and adult offenders to work with an elder who would conduct ho'oponopono for their families, as a form of alternative dispute resolution. The ho'oponopono is conducted in the traditional way, without court interference, with a practitioner picked by the family from a list of court-approved providers. Some native practitioners provide ho'oponopono to clients who otherwise might seek family counseling.

Freedom from karma

The site of the partially restored remains of the village of Koai'e in the Lapakahi State Historical Park of the island of Hawaii, North Kohala district. Beginning in the early 20th century, this village has been a center for lapa'au

In 1976 Morrnah Simeona, regarded as a healing priest or kahuna lapaʻau, adapted the traditional hoʻoponopono of family mutual forgiveness to the social realities of the modern day. For this she extended it both to a general problem solving process outside the family and to a psycho-spiritual self-help rather than group process.

Simeona's version is influenced by her Christian (Protestant and Catholic) education and her philosophical studies about India, China and Edgar Cayce. Like Hawaiian tradition she emphasizes prayer, confession, repentance, and mutual restitution and forgiveness. Unlike Hawaiian tradition, she describes problems only as the effects of negative karma, saying that "you have to experience by yourself what you have done to others." But that you are the creator of your life circumstances was common knowledge for the people of old as "things we had brought with us from other lifetimes. Any wrongdoing is memorized within oneself and mirrored in every entity and object which was present when the cause happened. As the Law of Cause and Effect predominates in all of life and lifetimes, the purpose of her version is mainly "to release unhappy, negative experiences in past reincarnations, and to resolve and remove traumas from the 'memory banks'.

Karmic bondages hinder the evolution of mind, so that "(karmic) cleansing is a requisite for the expansion of awareness". Using her 14-step-process would dissolve those bondages. She did not use mantras or conditioning exercises.

Her teachings include: there is a Divine Creator who takes care of altruistic pleas of Men; "when the phrase 'And it is done' is used after a prayer, it means Man's work ends and God's begins. "Self-Identity" signifies, example. during the ho'oponopono, that the three selves or aspects of consciousness are balanced and connected with the Divine Creator. Different from egoistic prayers, "altruistic prayers like ho'oponopono, where you also pray for the release of other entities and objects, reach the Divine plane or Cosmos because of their high vibrations. From that plane the Divine energy or "mana" would come, which would transform the painful part of the memory of the wrong actions in all participants to "Pure Light", on whatever plane they are existing; "all are set free" Through this transmutation in the mind the problems will lose their energy for physical effects, and healing or balancing is begun. In this sense, Simeona's mana is not the same as the traditional Polynesian understanding of mana.

Pacifica Seminars, founded by Morrnah Simeona, started the first Ho'oponopono seminars in Germany. Seminars are still held on a regular basis in Germany, Poland, France, and Denmark.

State of Zero

After Simeona's death in 1992, her former student and administrator, Ihaleakala Hew Len, co-authored a book with Joe Vitale called Zero Limits referring to Simeona's Ho'oponopono teachings. Len makes no claim to be a kahuna. In contrast to Simeona's teachings, the book brings the new idea that the main objective of Ho'oponopono is getting to the "zero state – it's where we have zero limits. No memories. No identity. To reach this state, which Len called 'Self-I-Dentity thru Ho'oponopono', includes using the mantra, "I love you. I'm sorry. Please forgive me. Thank you.

It is based on Len's idea of 100% responsibility, taking responsibility for everyone's actions, not only for one's own. If one would take complete responsibility for one's life, then everything one sees, hears, tastes, touches, or in any way experiences would be one's responsibility because it is in one's life. The problem would not be with our external reality, it would be with ourselves. Total Responsibility, according to Hew Len, advocates that everything exists as a projection from inside the human being. Another source of actively working Ho'oponopono is the book of haiku poems, Ho'oponopono Haiku. Tools as such are created by Ho'oponopono Practitioners from their journeys and experiences to zero state.

Who was Morrnah Simeona?
The last Queen and the birth of Morrnah Simeona
The last queen of Hawaii was Lilinokalani. In 1893 it was overthrown as a result of the US military invasion. The islands were annexed by the American government. The dethroned queen then attempted to translate Kumulipo - the ancient Hawaiian song of creation into English.

Thirty years later, Morrnah Nalamaku Simeona was born. Her father still remembered free Hawaii and belonged to the Queen's court. Morrnah Simeona was only a three-year-old girl when she revealed the unusual gift of healing. She was recognized as a healer in Kahuna Lapa'au. Morrnah did not receive any studies in this field, because she already had all the knowledge. It was born with her. She was an extraordinary child, to this *day there are legends about how she put her hand in the river, and the fish themselves came to her hand. When she was a mature woman, she got cancer, and the cancer turned out to be malignant. It was a turning point in her life and mission she had to accomplish on Earth. She recovered thanks to her abilities, knowledge, and application of the ancient Hawaiian Ho'oponopono process.*

The Foundation of Modern-day Ho'oponopono: Self-I-Dentity Through Ho'oponopono -" The Return Home."

Traditional Ho'ponopono, always run by Kahuna, was an important element of the life of the Hawaiian community - Ohana. No problem was dealt with there separately from the rest of the family and all people associated with it. However, Morrnah received Ho'oponopono directly from the Source, no one taught her the process.

Having experienced the power of Ho'oponopono, she decided to adapt it in such a way that it can be mastered and applied individually by every average person, even if he does not specialize in healing others. The challenge was to translate knowledge about this process into English.

Hawaiian is an agglutation language, it has no grammar, inflection, or syntax known to us, words are created in it by repeating syllables. For thousands of years, knowledge has been passed from mouth to mouth. The student could not change a single word or a single syllable. Thanks to this, the wisdom of the ancient Hawaiians survived. It owes its fidelity to its pure form to so many thousands of years. Most of the other ancient translations have been so distorted, repeatedly biased, that words have lost their power and true meaning.

Morrnah Simeona received spiritual guidance - this is how SELF-I-DENTITY THROUGH HO'OPONOPONO was created, - a process of purification and release in which man participates in direct connection with the Divine. In this process he finds his divine part, his self. Self-Identity is a return to the source, a return home. She made sure that the meaning of the words was not distorted. She offered the world the treasure of Love and Forgiveness in action. However, it was a gift dedicated not only to Westerners but a gift for the whole planet. it's a return to the source, a return home.

The Foundation of I - Freedom of The Cosmos

In the seventies, Morrnah Simeona founded "The Foundation of I - Freedom of the Cosmos", whose task was to promote Ho'oponopono. Its branch Pacifica Seminars was established in Europe. In 1980, Morrnah decided to leave Hawaii to share this gift with the Western world.

Morrnah lectured and taught in many states of North America, in Europe and other continents. Huge crowds of people took part in the meetings with her. During the visit to China, the number of participants exceeded fifteen thousand. Her works have been translated into several languages.

Self-I-Dentity through Ho'oponopono turned out to be such a deep-working and effective tool that it became interested in scientific institutions, medical institutions, universities as well as social and international organizations. The United Nations has invited her to lectures and training three times. She was also invited to meetings of the World Health Organization. Thanks to her, over 1.5 million people have learned the process around the world.

Allow Divinity in Your Life

Morrnah said that modern Westerners find it very difficult to put analytical thinking aside and get closer to their High Self. Westerners reach intellectual heights in many extreme ways. They pay for it with a sense of breakup and separation. By falling into the trap of analysis, they do not allow Divinity into their lives. Instead, they lead a constant struggle against all problems and adversities.

They do not allow divine energy to flow through them and act for their highest good. They don't want to entrust their problems to her, they prefer to fight alone. They cannot understand that the outside world is not an independent creation. They do not want to accept that it is only a reflection of their own interior. She always said that every stress, illness, or problem in relationships can be healed by working with yourself. Karmic Cleansing of Bonds.

Ho'oponopono recommended especially to healers, both as part of Western medicine and healers. She emphasized that we are all connected with karmic bonds, so it is highly recommended to cleanse such connections between the patient and the healer, because otherwise, they may become active in the process.

Morrnah was extremely humble, always obedient to divine guidance. She believed that if the patient came to her, then she is somehow responsible for his illness. That is why there are so frequent cases when a given healer should not simply work with a patient. You should always ask for permission to work with a specific person. If you do not get it and still undertake therapy, then you can take on its karmic burden.

Morrnah Nalamaku Simeona: Living Treasure of Hawaii.

In 1983, in recognition of her ability, work, and dedication to Hawaiian language, culture, and cultivating the art of healing and teaching Self-I-Dentity through Ho'oponopono, the authorities of the State of Hawaii and the Hongwanji Mission in Honolulu honored her with the title "Living Treasure of Hawaii". This was not the only honor she had received. The UN and the University of Cambridge published her biography, highlighting her contribution to society.

Morrnah's Visit to Poland and the Fall of the Berlin Wall.

Morrnah Nalamaku Simeona also visited Poland at a very important moment in the country. She taught Ho'oponopono and then went to Jasna Góra to cleanse and release the image of Our Lady of Częstochowa and the monastery treasury from the energy of regret and despair, whose immeasurable decks have accumulated there since the beginning. This place, so important for Poland, is its subconscious mind, in which the memory of painful, traumatic events is accumulated. For hundreds of years, huge amounts of grief, problems, ills, and tragedies have accumulated there, who went there asking for divine intercession.

The TV crew accompanied Morrnah Simeona on this extraordinary pilgrimage. During her stay in Poland, television showed her interview. Morrnah claimed that now that Poland's subconscious is cleared of the heaviest luggage, both Poland and Europe will finally be able to gain freedom. She predicted the breakdown of the ossified political system in Europe.

On October 14-15, Morrnah taught Ho'oponopono in Warsaw, after which she went to Częstochowa. Four weeks later, on November 9, 1989, the Berlin Wall fell.

Morrnah Simeona's Passing.

On November 11, 1992, Morrnah was in Germany. Suddenly she announced that her task on Earth had already been completed and she just went to bed.

She left with the same humility she went through her life.

CHAPTER 2.

Ho'oponopono is based on and constructed using the 12 Spiritual Laws of the Universe. These laws are, well, laws. They are always in force; immutable, impossible to circumvent. They are how the universe operates.

※ *The Law of Divine Oneness*

The universe is made of particles of energy. It is one great seething mass of particles. And every single one of them is connected to all the others. This means that every thing and every one are also connected, and all are part of this vast, limitless cosmic ocean. There is no separation. The idea that we are separate individuals is an illusion. We may feel that we are on our own while on this life experience, but when we die, the energy of our being-ness is returned to the whole.

There is no separation in the universe; we (and everything else) are all One, whether we are incarnated upon Earth or whether we are in our alternate natural state of pure energy. That means that love-energy is within you, prosperity-energy is within you, and health-energy is within you. You don't have to reach and struggle to bring good into your life, it is already there. You simply have to know it and let it manifest.

This is such a simple concept, yet so difficult to grasp. Everything you need and desire is already right here for you. Understanding the other 11 Universal Laws will enable you to get closer to this truth. Know that, in essence, there is only one single Universal Law, and this is it. The others are merely ways of breaking it down and explaining it.

"In the stillness of your presence, you can feel your own formless and timeless reality as the un manifested life that animates your physical form. You can then feel the same life deep within every other human and every other creature. You look beyond the veil of form and separation. This is the realization of oneness. This is love".   **Eckhart Tolle**

✶ *Law of Vibration*

Every particle vibrates and shimmies with energy. Nothing is at rest - whether it be the Earth herself, or the molecules of the desk you are sitting at. Everything has its own frequency, i.e. the speed at which it vibrates. Lower, negative energy vibrates more slowly than higher, positive energy. That doesn't mean one is better than the other; just that they are different.

While everything is part of the whole, that doesn't mean it's all the same. People, animals, objects, emotions, and thoughts all vibrate at different frequencies. And they influence each other. For example, you can't spend time with several high-vibrating, having-fun friends and not raise your vibration along with them. If your vibration stubbornly won't, or can't rise, then sooner or later, they will drift away from you. And, of course, it works the other way too. It depends which vibration is the strongest.

You can pinpoint your level of vibration by knowing how you are feeling at any given time. Abraham-Hicks has a useful, though not exhaustive, emotional scale:

Joy/Appreciation/Empowered/Freedom/Love
Passion/Inspired
Enthusiasm/Eagerness/Happiness/Contentment
Positive Expectation/Belief
Optimism

Hopefulness
Neutral
Boredom/Meh
Pessimism
Frustration/Irritation/Impatience
Overwhelm/Stress
Disappointment
Doubt
Worry
Blame
Discouragement/Depression
Anger
Revenge
Hatred/Rage
Jealousy
Insecurity/Guilt/Unworthiness
Fear
Grief
Deep depression
Despair
Powerlessness

Use this guide to move yourself up the emotional scale, thought-by-better-thought. It's just as easy to go up as it is to go down. In fact it is easier, because your natural tendency is to bob upward like a cork in water. A higher vibration means you attract higher vibration people and energy - just like a magnet. Lower vibrations repel the positive and attract negativity; higher vibrations attract the positive and repel lower vibrations.

"Everything in life is vibration." Albert Einstein

※ *Law of Correspondence*

The Law of Correspondence results from the Law of Divine Oneness. In essence, it means that patterns observed in the universe on a huge scale are also observed on the macro level. This results in harmony and agreement; cycles which are connected and related. Think how often the spiral pattern forms in nature. We see it in galaxies, on the faces of sunflowers and in the water that disappears down the waste outlet in our bath tubs. Every time we consult our horoscope, we are relying on the Law of Correspondence.

In essence, this Law is summed up by the words, "As above, so below." It means that the patterns of the universe are present in the smallest wee things as they are on a cosmic scale.

The Law of Correspondence ensures the universe works in harmony across the heavens, the earth, in the oceans, on the land, in your garden and in your body. It means that energy flows where it is supposed to. It mirrors itself in so many ways. This Law keeps everything in sync on the spiritual, physical and mental realms. This brings us back to Divine Oneness (as do all the Laws), that the one is part of the whole and is also part of the pattern of the universe.

For example, you can see this working on a personal scale. Remember a time when you felt depressed or bored or generally fed-up. You probably noticed that your mental level was reflected in your body. It's not possible to have a happy, active body under the direction of a miserable mind-set. Your body feels low on energy along with your low thoughts. And it can often, though not always, work the other way. A sick body will have an effect on your mind. Yet, a chronically ill person can teach and train themselves to raise their thought and emotional vibration and often find that their physical health improves. Understanding this, and working with the Universal Laws, means that you can be in harmony with the natural flow of energy, though you don't have to concern yourself too much with this one.

"As above, so below; as below, so above."-The Kybalion.

✳ Law of Attraction

By now everyone knows of the Law of Attraction, or 'like attracts like'. The Law of Attraction is tied to the law of Vibration in that things of the same vibrational frequency are attracted to each other. The key to working with LoA is to line your vibration (thoughts and emotions) up with whatever it is you want to come into your life. Unfortunately most of us think that that is all we need to do, but one needs to be aware of all 12 spiritual laws of the Universe in order to create a healthy and prosperous life.

This widely-touted Law simply explains that like energy attracts like energy. It is the result of the Law of Vibration. So much has been said about the Law of Attraction that we won't spend too much time on it here.

It's much more useful for you to be aware of the the Law of Vibration and where you are on the emotional scale. Once you do that, Law of Attraction does its fabulous stuff. Also the other Laws that we discuss here means that the Law of Attraction works consistently when you align yourself with them. So let the Law of Attraction look after itself.

That which is like unto itself is drawn. - Jerry and Esther Hicks

✳ *Law of Inspired Action*

Inextricably linked to the Law of Attraction is the Law of Inspired Action. This law states that to attain, achieve and attract what you want, you have to take inspired action toward those things. If a tiger needs to eat, she doesn't sit around waiting for a tasty treat to land at her feet, although some dogs we know do exactly that. The tiger takes action to achieve her aim of procuring food. The Law of Inspired Action helps you to facilitate what you desire. It doesn't have to be a great effort, just making a move in the right direction causes the Law of Vibration to kick in, which in turn, brings the Law of Attraction into play. Are you beginning to see how all these spiritual laws work together?

This is where you get to manipulate energy and put into motion your intention. This is an important Universal Law that many Law of Attraction enthusiasts forget about.

When you begin to play around with the emotional scale, and you are able to move yourself up a step at any given point in time, you will be able to explore the realm of intent. You are already using intent, of course, but you may not be using it to your best advantage.

The Law of Inspired Action kicks in when you have deliberately formed an intent. Your enthusiasm and desire for the intent to translate into a tangible result causes you to take action, the first step. When you do this, and continue to do it toward the manifestation of your intent, Universal Laws are bound to work in your favor.

A real-life example is when a seed is caused to germinate by temperature and soil conditions. The seed has the intent to germinate; a change (action/energy) in its environment causes germination to occur.

Take the first step in faith. You don't have to see the whole staircase. Just take the first step. - Dr Martin Luther King Jr.

✳ **Law of Perpetual Transmutation of Energy**

The Law of Transmutation means that all energy: that which is constant motion due to the Law of Vibration, is also in constant flux. From the stars and planets to the cells in our bodies. It's true that some changes aren't visible because the particles simply reform into what they were previously. Higher vibrations are able to 'encourage' low vibrations to speed up. For instance, let's say you are feeling low, if you get outside, breathe, absorb the positive energy of nature, you will always feel better than you did before, even if it's a temporary state. And again, you can connect this to the Law of Action and help things along.

This Law is another result of the Law of Vibration. As the particles and waves of the Universe, flow and change and vibrate, they change the particles alongside them. Everything is in motion. Nothing ever stays still. Even the table in front of you; it's molecules are vibrating constantly. However, the physical laws of the Universe means that certain molecules are anchored to each other, meaning that their visible appearance doesn't change. Otherwise, we'd be in a constant state of disorder and chaos. Another way to think about this is that 'thoughts become things'. Everything around you was a thought before it became manifest - your coffee mug, your TV even your puppy. And yes, rocks, trees and flowers were also 'thoughts', though not in the same way as we 'think'.

When energy is converted from passive to active energy, it is transmuted to other materials or changed to other forms. Transmission/transmutation of the forms of energy are a continuing process of the material universe.

The Light Shall Set You Free - Dr. Norma Milanovich & Dr. Shirley McCain

※ *The Law of Cause and Effect*

The Universal Law of Cause and Effect is probably the easiest to understand. It states that for every action there is some kind of reaction. In the physical realm this is pretty obvious, yet it happens in the spiritual realm also. Remember that energy is everywhere. It's what Wallace Wattles called, 'the thinking substance'. It fills space, it fills us. There is no such thing as an energy vacuum. Each deed, thought and emotion is a movement of energy and thus has an effect on energy around you.

You will be familiar with Newton's Third Law from your science class at school: "For every action, there is an equal and opposite reaction." Well, it's the same in the quantum realm of universal energy. Every thought you think sends out a wave of vibrational energy, starting right within your own body. You witness this in action all the time. People who think of poverty and lack, live a life of poverty and lack. People who see themselves as incapable, will life a life of incapacity. It's the same with emotions; after all thoughts and emotions are inextricably linked.

Therefore, you do yourself no favors when you wallow in negative thoughts and emotions. You can't create a perfect life if you are always feeling stressed or rushed. In the same way, your words and deeds are also impressed upon universal energy. If you carry out a task with a feeling of resentment, the universe responds accordingly. If you help someone in a spirit of generosity and love, again, the universe responds accordingly. The Law of Cause and effect is inevitably connected to the following law...

Through the law of cause and effect we choose our destiny. Moreover, we are our own prophets for we constantly project our future state by the seeds we plant in the present. – Cheryl Canfield

※ *The Law of Compensation*

The Law of Compensation works in tandem with the Law of Cause and Effect. In a nutshell, it means that you will receive what you put out. This is not just to do with riches and wealth. Riches can be a punishment as well as a reward. A person who wins the lottery may not be reaping benefits of a good life, but be in the process of creating their own downfall. There are countless examples that show that wealth is not necessarily an indicator of a happy and fulfilled life. So, the Law of Compensation is a little like Karma. You reap what you sow. Good, bad, positive or negative are not factors. The Law of Compensation just is.

The Law of Compensation is the other side of the cause and effect coin. The Law of Compensation is the result of your thoughts, words, deeds, etcetera. You reap what you sow. It's a great law to work with once you understand that you are creating with all your energetic intentions. When you realize that those stray thoughts have real results, then you begin to understand what Abraham-Hicks means when they talk about their interpretation: The Law of Deliberate Creation. If you can understand these two important aspects of how Divine Oneness works - the Law of Cause and Effect and the Law of Compensation, then you can begin to shape your life as if it were soft clay in your hands.

When you understand the law of divine compensation, you realize that in the presence of spiritual consciousness, there is more than enough compensation for any diminishment in materiality. –
Marianne Williamson

✳ Law of Relativity

The Universal Law of Relativity shows us that nothing can be judged; deemed good or bad, until it is compared with something else. The Law of Relativity works for us and against us constantly, and it is always a good (see what we did there?) thing to remind ourselves of it each time we slip into judging mode. This person is bad because we compare his or her behavior to what is currently socially acceptable. That person is good because he or she is more altruistic than their neighbor. You can't tell the size of a star without comparing it to others and judging the amount of light it emits. You can't know how wealthy you are unless you measure yourself against the wealth of other people. In non-judgment and comparison, a 'thing' just 'is'.

The Law of Relativity (not to be confused with Einstein's Theory of Relativity) could also be named, 'the law of comparison'. Until one thing is compared to another it can't be assessed, judged, or measured. It's about the relationship of something to something else. The Law of Relativity acts as a force of spiritual resistance. In physical life, it would be called a challenge.

For example, a child runs alone along a 100 yard track. We just see a child running. Yet if the child is running alongside nine other children, we are able to judge his or her performance. Should the child come second, or last in the race, then that is a challenge for him or her to do better. In the same way, we are spiritually forced to grow and evolve. If we are never challenged, we would simply drift along. We'd never accomplish anything. We would never improve our understanding. We wouldn't bother doing anything. And we'd certainly never have world-class athletes.

Problems, obstacles, lack, illness, relationships, all help to challenge our perspective by letting us compare what is with what we'd prefer. Thus we change and mature. We learn to open our hearts; we learn it's okay to admit defeat, or to ask for help. All this pushes us towards the higher realms of consciousness and spiritual attainment. The Universal Law of Relativity helps us to know our true selves.

The very beginning of creation gave rise to the law of duality—light and darkness, good and evil—the law of relativity necessary to divide the One into the many. – Paramahansa Yolanda

※ *Law of Polarity*

Everything that exists has an opposite. You can't discern darkness without having known light. You can't know happiness without feeling sad. Contrast enables us to experience. Imagine picking up a stick. On one end is joy, on the other end, fear. It's your decision where to hold the stick. It's all on a spectrum and you get to choose how you pick up that stick.

The Law of Polarity could be described as 'opposites'. Day and night, good and evil. However, it's really important to understand that these polarities are the same thing, they are not different but contrasting. Light and dark are simply at different frequencies on the vibrational scale. Similarly, good and bad. What the Law of Polarity helps you with is understanding where on that vibrational scale you are focusing your attention. Your emotions are really important indicators of the Law of Polarity. This brings us right back to the emotional guidance scale. It is impossible to change your emotional frequency from regret to joy in one movement or thought. The Universal Law of Polarity simply won't allow that to happen. It has to be done in increments. Of course you can skip stages; you could easily move from hopeful and optimistic to passionate and inspired. And, like the chutes in Chutes and Ladders, you could slip down the scale pretty quickly. However, the key point to understand about the Law of Polarity is that you can control the balance. You are able to recognize when you are feeling less-than-good, and take steps to rectify it. You can sense when you are slipping down the scale, and do something about it. You can also see when you are improving, and knowing that helps you to feel even better.

"A fish will not truly learn to enjoy water, without gasping for air." — Markus W.

✳ *Law of Rhythm*

The Universal Law of Rhythm is also the Law of Perpetual Motion. It means that everything moves in cycles: orbits, tides and even politics. Empires rise and fall, economies prosper and fail. Seasons change, the Wheel of the Year turns. We're all moving to the rhythm of life... and death.

Also known as 'ebb and flow', the Law of Rhythm is manifested on the back of the Law of Polarity. In the natural world, every time something swings too far in one direction, it's balanced out by a swing in the opposite direction. Think of changes in the season, tidal current, moon cycles. Even the financial markets work on this principle. We can also relate this to the Law of Cause and Effect, and indeed all the other universals laws. Before this current era of 'artificial life', humans were extremely attuned to the natural cycles of the universe and used them as guidance for their lives. These same rhythms occur in the ebb and flow of unseen energy and you have probably felt it in your own body and emotional balance. Begin to pay more attention to the 'rhythms of life' and learn when to direct the swing yourself and when to go with the flow.

"Everything flows, out and in; everything has its tides; all things rise and fall; the pendulum-swing manifests in everything; the measure of the swing to the right is the measure of the swing to the left; rhythm compensates."- The Kybalion.

✻ *Law of Gender*

The Law of Gender is the manifestation of Yin and Yang. It is another form of the Law of Polarity. This is not limited to what sex a person is; it is the balance of the Divine Masculine and Feminine within. Everything has this dual quality and each extreme has its corresponding opposite. It is two pieces of a jigsaw. Night and day. It's interconnected with all the other Universal Laws.

This is another manifestation of the Law of Polarity. It's important to understand that, in this context, gender does not just mean sex, although sex is is part of the Universal Law of Gender. What it means is that there is a Divine Feminine and Divine Masculine throughout the Universe. Without these two 'polarities' there would be no creation. Simplistically, you could think of a piece of paper as feminine, and the artist who wields the brush as masculine. You need both a support (paper, canvas, etc.) and an agent of change (artist with a brush, pen, etc.) to create a work of art.

Other, and often erroneous ways, of describing the Universal Law of Gender are 'passive and active', or 'negative and positive'. It's time we thought up better words for the Law of Gender. You can't really work with this law apart from understanding a little how it works. You can't change anything about it - it just is. Humans have always been able to discern that this Divine principle is in everything. Some languages assign gender to certain words. In French, dog is always masculine and cat is feminine. We see nature as feminine, and the Moon as feminine, and the Sun is masculine. Atoms are made up of masculine and feminine components - it's what holds them together to form an overall neutral structure. Gender in the broader, over-arching sense is the glue that holds the whole Universe together in Divine Oneness.

Masculine energy is attracted to feminine principles (and) when they unite; they form a union that assures the creative process will be realized. The Light Shall Set You Free - Dr. Norma Milanovich & Dr. Shirley McCain

CHAPTER 3.

Dr. Ihaleakala Hew Len, or Dr Hew Len as he's better known, is probably the most widely known teacher of Ho'oponopono since Joe Vitale wrote the book Zero Limits with him to introduce The State of Zero that builds on Self I-Dentity through Ho'oponopono.

Dr. Ihaleakala Hew Len, Zero Limits. "Be your own guru"

Dr. Hew Len studied with, and taught around the world with, Morrnah Simeona the developer of Self I-Dentity through Ho'oponopono for many years.

Although now retired he is actively involved with The Foundation of I, Inc. and IZI LLC as Chairman Emeritus working with Kamaile Rafaelovich another long time student of Morrnah Simeona.

Dr. Ihaleakala Hew Len and Kamaile Rafaelovich are featured in the wonderful books BLUE ICE: The Relationship with The Self: MsKr SITH® Conversations, Book 1 and BLUE ICE: Memories and Relationships: MsKr SITH® Conversations, Book 2 that are based on transcripts from radio shows that they participated in.

Dr. Hew Len wrote "Who's in Charge" a document that serves as foundational reading for students who plan on taking SITH courses available through IZI LLC.

"The only task in your life and mine is the restoration of our Identities - our Minds - back to their original state of void or zero."

~ Ihaleakala Hew Len, Ph.D.

Dr. Hew Len, the Teacher of the healing system Ho'oponopono

Enter Dr. Hew Len

One day, a newly appointed clinical psychologist, a Dr. Stanley Hew Len, arrived at the ward. The nurses rolled their eyes, bracing themselves for one more guy that was going to bug them with new theories and proposals to fix the horrid situation, and who would walk away as soon as things became unpleasant,

around a month later, usually. However, this new doctor wouldn't do anything like that. Actually he didn't seem to be doing anything in particular, except just coming in and being always cheerful and smiling, in a very natural, relaxed way. He wasn't even particularly early in arriving every morning. From time to time he would ask for the files of the inmates. He never tried to see them personally, though. Apparently he just sat in an office, looked at their files, and to members of the staff who showed an interest, he would tell them about a weird thing called Ho'oponopono. Little by little things started to change in the hospital. One day somebody would try again to paint those walls and they actually stayed painted, making the environment more palatable. The gardens started being taken care of, some tennis courts were repaired and some prisoners that up until then would never be allowed to go outside started playing tennis with the staff. Other prisoners would be allowed not to be shackled any more, or would receive less heavy pharmacological drugs. More and more obtained permission to go outside unshackled, without causing

Ihaleakalā Hew Len, Ph. D.

trouble to the hospital's employees.

    In the end, the atmosphere changed so much that the staff was not on sick leave any more. Actually, more people than needed wished now to work there. Prisoners started gradually to be released. Dr. Hew Len worked there close to four years. In the end, there remained only a couple of inmates that were relocated somewhere else and the clinic for the mentally insane criminals had to close. I had heard about the doctor and I had developed an instant frenzy, a desperate need to learn what he had done with the crazy criminals, so I grabbed an article of the internet on my phone and rushed home and started reading on a bigger screen, and I didn't stop until the last word. What did Dr. Hew Len do to the patients, how did he treat them that the results were so spectacular? He didn't do anything. Not a thing to them nor with them, except looking at their files. He only tried to heal himself, applying an old, traditional community problem-solving system from Hawaii, called Ho'oponopono, adapted to individuals by his Teacher, the late Hawaiian sage Morrnah Nalamaku Simeona. And what was he doing to himself? In his own words: "I was simply healing the part of me that created them". Actually, he used to sit in his office and look at the patients' files. While perusing them, he would feel something, a pain, an empathy. Then he started the healing on himself, taking full responsibility for what was going on with a given patient. That's how those people got better, because their doctor had the strange view that it was himself who needed the healing, not them. Ho'oponopono, Simply put, Ho'oponopono is based on the knowledge that anything that happens to you or that you perceive, the entire world where you live is your own creation and thus, it is entirely your responsibility. A hundred percent, no exceptions.

Your boss is a tyrant? It's your responsibility. Your children are not good students? It's your responsibility. There are wars and you feel bad because you are a good person, a pacifist? The war is your responsibility. You see that children around the world are hungry and malnourished if not starving? Their wont is your responsibility. No exceptions. Literally, the world is your world, it is your creation. As Dr. Hew Len points out: didn't you notice that whenever you experience a problem you are there? It's your responsibility doesn't mean it's your fault, it means that you are responsible for healing yourself in order to heal whatever or whoever it is that appears to you as a problem. It might sound crazy, or just plain metaphorical, that the world is your creation. But if you look carefully, you will realize that whatever you call the world and perceive as the world is your world, it is the projection of your own mind. If you go to a party you can see how in the same place, with the same light, the same people, the same food, drink, music and atmosphere, some will enjoy themselves while others will be bored, some will be overenthusiastic and some depressed, some will be talkative and others will be silent. The "out there" for every one of them seems the same, but if one were to connect their brains to machines immediately it would show how different areas of the brain would come alive, how different perceptions there are from one person to the next. So even if they apparently share it, the "out there" is not the same for them, let alone their inner world, their emotions.

There are seminars where they teach you many tricks to help this process, but according to Joe Vitale, Dr. Hew Len himself uses the simplest of the formulas from Ho'oponopono. Whenever a matter arises, and they arise incessantly, adressing the Divine within you, you only have to say: I love You, I'm sorry, Please forgive me, Thank You. That we can obtain big things from Ho'oponopono has already been shown: the healing of an entire ward of insane criminals seems far more difficult a task than any of our personal troubles. There are, no doubt, piles of testimonies from practitioners. Dr. Hew Len says, however: this is not fast food. The cleaning of memories requires a lot of concentration and persistence and is an unending job. But the result is what he calls

Zero Limits, a state where one is free from the past, and suffused with Divine Intelligence and love.

If Dr Hew Len Was Able To Clear Out a Criminally Insane Ward Without Therapy, Then How Can We Impact Our Personal Lives Using The Powerful Problem Solving Process Of Ho'oponopono? Dr Hew Len worked at the Hawaii State hospital in the high security ward for the criminally insane from 1983 to 1987, where he cured and entire ward of criminally mentally ill patients using the simple ancient Hawaiian healing method of Ho'oponopono. During that time, Dr Hew Len didn't do any therapy on the patients. He would walk through the ward, and review the patient's files, not for the purpose of therapy but to see what there was there for him to clean up. So if Dr Hew Len didn't work on the patients, how was it that he was able to cure the entire ward of criminally mentally ill patients? He always kept in mind that every one, including the patients in that ward were all really creations of The Divine. And in being so, they were all perfect beings with perfect minds in that they all were an exact replication of The Divine; represented by the Void and Infinite. Given that information: What is a problem? According to Ho'oponopono, a problem is a memory replaying in the subconscious mind.

When Dr Hew Len did Ho'oponopono in the hospital, he would ask himself: "What is going on in me that I experience the hospital / situation in such a way?" - Being that Dr Hew Len knew that in essence he was perfect, and that the criminals in essence were also perfect - he asked himself: "What is this problem going on?" Dr Hew Len used the following analogy to explain was the problem was: "Imagine the mind is like a canvas, and on that canvas of the mind is painted a stain, and that stain is a memory." - "The stain is left there on the sub-conscious mind, and when it gets triggered, it replays a past experience." So a problem is a memory replaying a past experience. Ho'oponopono is an appeal to The Divinity to cancel the memories that replay as problems. And as Dr Hew Len would move through the ward, he would ask himself: "What is going on in me that I am experiencing these problems?"

Dr Hew Len would continuously clean the memories in his sub-conscious mind that would come up as he went through each patient's file, looking within himself at what came up, and what he needed to let go of.

When Dr Hew Len arrived at the hospital every one of the seclusion rooms were occupied with violent patients, but as he let go the memories and feelings in him, within a year and a half, all of the seclusion rooms had been shut down, and patients were starting to be able to take care of themselves.

Knowing that all memories are shared, Dr Hew Len worked on what ever was going on in him that he experienced as the criminals being the way they were. As Dr Hew Len asked Divinity to erase those memories, he got clear, the patients got better, and over the four years that he was at the hospital, many of the patients went home, and eventually the ward was actually shut down.

As Dr Hew Len incessantly did his cleaning on what ever was going on in him, the shared memory he had with the patients, that he experienced as problems in the ward, they got cancelled in him, he got clear, and the patients in the ward stayed for much shorter periods of time.

Dr Hew Len points out that that a major problem with therapists is that they keep thinking that they are in practice to save people, when actually; they are in practice to get clear themselves. Dr Hew Len says that as we heal the memories that we share with other people, those people get cancelled, and people just get better. Before Dr Hew Len came on board in that ward, the psychologists would last for approximately one month, and then they would quit. But Dr Hew Len just worked on himself, and what ever was going on in him before he went in each day to the ward, while he was there, and after he left each day. He constantly worked on the common data that he shared with the patients and that he experienced as problems.

About a year later, people started asking: "What is going on that the ward is so quiet?"

It was because Dr Hew Len was only interested in being 100% responsible for what ever was going on in his life. He was only interested in being clear so that his life was peaceful, with less stress and less confusion.

And today, that ward is no longer in use.

Dr Hew Len points out that the bottom line is that when ever there is a problem that we notice, we are always there. So Dr Hew Len constantly asked The Divinity to make amends for whatever he had in the common, and that he was experiencing as problems with the patients in that ward.

He says that the only reason that he exists is because "peace begins with me", and although he still stumbles a lot, that is what he practices.

With Ho'oponopono, we are taking responsibility for common memories we share with other people.

Research shows that at any given moment, there are more than 11 million bits of information going on, and yet, we are only aware of 15 bits of them. And those are the bits that we make judgments on. But we do not know what is going on. So we say to The Divinity: "If there is something going on in me that I am experiencing people in a certain way, I would like to let go of them."

By letting go, we change the world in us, and that in turn causes the whole world to change. Being 100% responsible is a tough road to travel, because the intellect is so insistent. Whenever a problem comes to us, our intellect always looks for someone or something to blame. We keep looking outside of ourselves for the source of our problems.

But the source is always inside us.

Dr Hew Len's teacher, Morrnah Simeona taught that: "We are only here to bring peace to our own life, and if we bring peace to our own life, everything around us will find its own place, its own rhythm and peace", and that is what Ho'oponopono is all about. When ever Dr Hew Len deals with the clients that email him from all over the world, he only looks within himself, and asks himself: "What is going on in me that they should express /

experience this problem?" He asks himself: "What is it in me that I have to cancel?" He points out that he does not know what to cancel in him, but The Divinity in him, who created him and knows everything does. Dr Hew Len appeals to that Source in him to cancel what ever is going on in him that he experiences as problems.

Dr Hew Len says that Ho'oponopono teaches us not to be intrusive in other people's lives, and give them advice, but when we experience other people as problems, we must ourselves: "What is going on in me that I am experiencing this?"

He makes the point that the mind never understands things as they are, but rather gets a replication of it. He says that the mind has a model of the way things work, but that is not what is really going on, because if the mind really knew what was going on, it would not experience problems.

He continued by saying that decisions are made for us before we ever decide them, because there are millions of unconscious memories going on in our sub-conscious minds all the time, and that these memories make decisions for us. And since we are not aware of the memories, we need to talk to Divinity who is aware of them, and is the only one who can cancel them.

So moment by moment, as we practice the Ho'oponopono process, we are canceling the memories in our sub-conscious mind by saying to The Divine: "I don't know why I am experiencing this, but if I have a common problem with other people, I would like to make amends for it."

It is imperative to realize that the person who practices the Ho'oponopono process is not doing the healing, rather the Ho'oponopono is the process of allowing The Divinity who created everything and knows everything, to cancel the memories that we experience as problems.

What we are doing with the Ho'oponopono cleaning is putting everything back into its natural order.

Dr Hew Len says that if we are prepared to be 100% responsible first, and get 100% at peace with ourselves, everything else will get into perfect alignment with themselves and The Divinity. We all have common shared histories, which are all inter-connected.

The Ho'oponopono process only takes one person: - "Peace begins with me, and no one else." At that hospital in Hawaii, because Dr Hew Len cleaned himself, everyone got well and as he did the Ho'oponopono process, patients were able to take care of themselves.

Dr Hew Len says that what everyone wants is to be in tune with themselves, and only when they are, will they be able to fulfill the destiny for which they came, he stresses that we need to be clear that the mind is perfect. - What is not perfect is the data and memories that our mind carries, and with Ho'oponopono, that is what we are working on. We are working on canceling common memories.

Whenever Dr Hew Len talks to people, he only looks for the common memory that they share, that he may not even be aware of (remember, our conscious mind is only aware of 15 bits of information out of 11 million bits). And it only takes one person prepared to be 100% responsible to erase the shared memory.

Ho'oponopono is only about looking at ourselves by cleaning the garbage we share in common with other people that creates problems for us. Dr Hew Len said that he enjoys when people are being rude to him, because he knows that it is the data which is causing them to be that way, and he is looking for data to erase, and the best data to erase is bad data. The definition of Ho'oponopono is to correct and error, and the error is corrected by saying: "I Love You", "I'm sorry", "Please forgive me" and "Thank You" to The Divine, in order to allow The Divinity to void and cancel the data (memories in the sub-conscious mind) that we experience as problems.

By doing the different Ho'oponopono processes, I am asking The Divinity to cancel programs (memories) in me, so that they too get cancelled in other people. I only need to look at what is going on in me, which I have in common with other people. I am willing to be 100% responsible, because I can only depend on myself to bring peace to my own life, because that is my responsibility.

Dr Hew Len says that if we are not doing our cleaning all the time, then someone who is already unhappy may show up in our existence, and that may cause us to be stuck with their grief. If someone shows up angry in my experience, I take 100% responsibility by asking myself: "What is going on in me, that I need to let go of, that this experience is coming up?" I look at what is the problem (memories) in me that is causing this situation that I can have cancelled by The Divinity?

I need to always be cleaning, because I want to prevent any problems from surfacing, if it is correct that they are prevented. However, Dr Hew Len points out that some problems have to show up. Why? That is something that only The Divinity knows, but the Ho'oponopono process is about preventing.

Ho'oponopono is about letting go and trusting, because outcomes are the job of the intellect, and according to Dr Hew Len, intentions are what kills people. Dr Hew Len says that all expectations are just memories replaying, and that nothing in life happens by accident. It is The Divinity who is orchestrating events, and our job is to be at peace.

Dr Hew Len said that if we insist on setting goals we need to be constantly cleaning so that we will be willing to let go and allow our life to go in the way it needs to go. If we are inflexible, and have our mind set on only one goal, then we will miss many opportunities (inspirations) that shows up from The Divine.

The only way I can be at peace is by tuning into myself, and by doing that, I am contributing to the welfare of all the people around me. I do Ho'oponopono for myself, because I want to be at peace, and because I know that as long as I am at peace with myself, I will notice that everyone around me is peaceful. So whenever I notice anything that I perceive as a problem, I say to myself: "What is going on in me that I need to let go of?"

Dr Hew Len teaches that people only show up in our lives to show us that we are either on track (or not) in our own lives. Most of the time we don't know if we are (or not), so we constantly need to clean, he goes on to say, that trying to help people by talking to them doesn't help. With Ho'oponopono I bring peace to myself, so that everyone around me can be at peace with themselves.

Before Dr Hew Len eats anything, he says in his mind to the food: "I love You...If I am bringing anything to this situation that would cause me to feel ill as I am eating you; - it is not you. It is not even me. It is something that triggers that I am willing to be responsible for." When there is a memory replaying, and we are in grief, we do things that we ordinarily wouldn't do, but if we are willing to work on that memory, we can cancel it. He practices Ho'oponopono during every breath that he takes. He says that he is willing to work on his memories, because if he doesn't, he will be sick, unhappy, confused and blameful, and that is not a place where he wants to be.

A Message from

DR. IHALEAKALA HEW LEN IS FULLY RETIRED. HE HAS ASKED US, HIS ZERO-WISE AND CEEPORT CLEANING TEAM, TO CONTINUE HIS LEGACY ONLINE. AND SO IT IS DONE. AS ALWAYS WE ARE HERE FOR YOU.

The only purpose in your life and mine is the restoration of our Identity—our Mind—back to its original state of void or zero (Buddha), of purity of heart (Jesus) and of blank (Shakespeare) through nonstop cleaning.

It is in the void, at zero, Divine Love resides, providing inspiration for perfect relationships, perfect health and perfect wealth.

The responsibility and the function of the Conscious Mind (Intellect) is to initiate the cleaning, to care for the Subconscious, teach it the cleansing process and to ask Divinity for directions.

The Conscious Mind is clueless as to what memories are replaying (11,000,000 per second) in the Subconscious. ONLY DIVINE LOVE CAN TRANSMUTE TOXIC MEMORIES TO PURE ENERGIES. DIVINE LOVE IS THE ONLY SOURCE OF INSPIRATION AND ENLIGHTENMENT!

The Conscious Mind does not perform these functions!

The Subconscious, as the super computer, is the key in the Self I-Dentity through Ho'oponopono cleansing process. If loved and cared for, the Subconscious becomes an ally, cleansing nonstop even as we sleep.

I wish you and your family, relatives and ancestors Peace beyond understanding.

Peace of I,

CHAPTER 4

Why you should practice ho'oponopono?

According to Dr. James' research, people who practice ho'oponopono have a better experience with forgiving others and are less likely to carry around the burden of un-forgiveness. The intentional element of gratitude also does a body good.

A 2012 study published in Personality and Individual Differences found that people with more gratitude led healthier lives than those who experience gratitude less frequently. People with more gratitude exercise more often and practice self-care on a more regular basis. Quite simply, if you live with more gratitude, then you tend to take better care of yourself.

Gratitude also improves your psychological health. Robert Emmons is one of the foremost researchers on gratitude on mental health. In a series of studies, he and his colleagues helped people cultivate gratitude and then examined the effects. After examining more than 1,000 people from all age groups, they found that people who practice gratitude not only have stronger immune systems and fewer aches and pains, but also a higher level of positive emotions, more joy, more optimism and are more outgoing than those who don't.

Unsurprisingly, Emmons has also found that gratitude helps us forgive more and feel less lonely and isolated. As he states, "gratitude is a social emotion." He views gratitude as a way to strengthen relationships, which is the primary reason for ho'oponopono.

Time to practice ho'oponopono and see and feel the benefits.

Ho'oponopono is a practice from Hawaii that revolves around forgiveness and connection. "Ho'o" means "to make" and "pono" means "right." The repetition of pono means to make "doubly right," according to Matthew B. James, MA, Ph.D., and president of Kona University.

The process differs depending on its heritage. As Dr. James explains, the state of Hawaii is divided into four counties with city and county governments. The reason behind this, he says, is the state was once divided into several kingdoms, with Hawai'i, Maui, O'ahu, and Kauai being the largest. Despite how geographically close the islands are from one another, communication could cease between kingdoms for hundreds of years, so the *practice of ho'oponopono evolved a little differently in each place.*

Some islands practiced ho'oponopono face to face, while others used a mediator as communication between the two parties. Ho'oponopono can also be practiced alone as a mindfulness exercise. It is the latter method that most non-Hawaiians use today.

How do we start incorporating Ho'oponopono into our own lives?

As the Chinese proverb says: "A Journey of 1000 miles begins with one step." Dr Hew Len always drinks blue solar water. As he drinks, he is petitioning Divinity to cancel memories he shares with other people. As he petitions Divinity, he doesn't know which memories are being cancelled.

Ho'oponopono has cleaning processes which include food, breathing and exercise. Dr Hew Len says that his whole life is geared to fulfill the purpose for which he came to fulfill - and that is to clear his mind of problems (memories) so that he can be what The Divine created him to be - pure in heart.

He also pointed out that the word Aloha is a profound word which means: Be in the presence (Alo) of The Divine *(ha). He says that when we say Aloha to someone, we are acknowledging that that person is Divinity personified.*

Dr Hew Len wants to lead the Ho'oponopono lifestyle, so he continuously cleans, acknowledging that everything in his life is Divinity personified, and he confesses that Ho'oponopono is tough to do. He says there isn't a day that goes by that he isn't annoyed, irritable, saying how come?, or thinking, but at least he is aware of it, and as soon as he realizes that he has slipped, he gets back into the cleaning. He says that there isn't a day that goes by that he doesn't stumble.

Strawberries and blueberries are wonderful problem solving processes that petition Divinity to cancel our problem causing memories. The "I love You" prayer and the blue solar water are all used in conjunction.

Dr Hew Len also pointed out that the word Hawaii means "The breath and water of The Divine". Dr Hew Len says that the "Ha" process is a canceling process and is simple to do.

The process is done by breath In, mentally count to 7, Hold for 7 mental counts, Exhale - mentally count to 7, Hold - mentally count to 7. Repeat the process 7 times.

Dr Hew Len says that Ho'oponopono is a process where we say to The Divine: "I'm sorry" (repentance);

"Please forgive me" (forgiveness); and *"Thank You"* (transmutation).

Only The Divinity can reach down into the sub-conscious mind and take the problem memories and neutralize them, and then remove the memory into storage, and leave the mind blank. And now that the mind is at peace again since there is no memory or problems. Once the mind goes into this state of emptiness and peacefulness, Divinity comes through with inspiration, and as the inspiration comes in, the canceling / transmutation of memories takes place, which only The Divine can do.

Ho'oponopono is all about being 100% responsible.

With all these processes, I am saying to The Divinity; *"I'm sorry for whatever is going on in me that I am experiencing the world to be a certain way."* The Divinity receives the petition, and then it is at The Divinity's discretion to then send down spiritual and mental energy into the sub-conscious mind and begin to neutralize the problem memory. The neutralized energy is then pulled out and stored, and the mind is left empty, and is then ready to receive inspiration from The Divinity.

Dr Hew Len says that we are all Divine Beings, but the mind can only serve one master at one time. It can either serve memories replaying problems, or it can serve Divinity which is inspirations. The intellect has a choice: It can either be run by problems, or it can be run by inspiration.

Dr Hew Len said that we must look out for having expectations in our life. He said that the cleaning has nothing to do with expectations. We are not cleaning to save anyone's life. Why we are cleaning is to have whatever is perfect and right happen to us peacefully. Cleaning is done to get the circumstances that are perfect and right for us. But we don't know what that is. Only The Divine knows.

The Ho'oponopono cleaning is profound because we are dealing directly with The Divine, and The Divine can do its job perfectly. We can't tell Divinity what results we can from our cleaning. Our only responsibility is to say: "I'm sorry and please forgive me". And Divinity's responsibility is to do whatever.

"Hawaii - the word Ha means "inspiration. Wai is "water' and I is 'the Divine". Hawaii is the breath and the water of the Divine.

The word itself is a cleansing process, so when I am anywhere and I check- I say, for example, before I go into the room.

"What is it that I need to clear that I don't know? I have no idea what's going on, so what is it?"

So, if I apply a cleaning process that is called "Hawaii," it will get data that I am not even aware of and take me back to zero".

"Embracers inspire seeing differently, clearing toxic memories and releasing rebel powers in your soul.

Wearing an "Embracer" allows the cleaning to take place continuously, embracing memories of pain and suffering with love, gratitude and forgiveness, releasing them back to nothing. This constant cleaning allows the mind to return to zero,

restoring the soul to pure light and love.

Only at zero is love renewed and divine inspiration becomes possible."

The practice of ho'oponopono centers around four phrases:

I am sorry.
Please forgive me.
I love you.
Thank you.
The practice begins with "I am sorry" and "please forgive me" as a way a cleaning the practitioner of negative feelings. It may feel counter-intuitive to start this way, especially if you don't really want to forgive someone, but starting off like this can be viewed as something you're doing for yourself. As the ubiquitous quote says, "Resentment is like taking poison and waiting for the other person to die."

Allow the first half of the practice to clear that resentment and hurt. Letting go and forgiving someone does not excuse their behavior. It simply opens you to the possibility of letting go of the pain. It is in this spirit that you should practice ho'oponopono.

The next two phrases, "I love you" and "thank you," add gratitude and love to the practice. Gratitude has been shown to improve not only your mental health but also your physical health.

As an individual practice, ho'oponopono can be done through meditation or as a journaling or letter-writing exercise. To whom you address your plea for forgiveness depends on what you need at the time.

You can use ho'oponopono to forgive yourself or someone in your life. You can also use it to boost your gratitude for the world in its entirety, or your local community. Its universality makes ho'oponopono an exercise that you can practice daily in a different way.

※ *How to try ho'oponopono as a writing exercise*

As a journaling or letter-writing exercise, simply settle into a cozy spot where you won't be disturbed and visualize to whom you'd like to address the practice. Begin by writing "I am sorry" as many times as you would like. If you're unsure, I often recommend writing it out three times as a nice target.

Continue with the next three phrases: "Please forgive me," "I love you" and "thank you." Sit with each phrase for a bit and really absorb them. When you are done, you can even journal about the experience and the thoughts that have come to the surface for you. You may not want to send that letter, but the process is valuable in itself.

✳ How to mix ' with meditation

Another way to practice ho'oponopono is through meditation. You can simply add the phrases to your meditation as you would during an affirmation or mantra meditation, or you can follow the simple script below:

Begin by sitting comfortably on your cushion and close your eyes.

Taking notice of your breath, begin by visualizing yourself surrounded by beautiful, healing light. You might even imagine the concept of safety as a color. Drape yourself in this color.

Next, draw to mind the person or people to whom you'd like to extend forgiveness. If the session is for yourself, then imagine looking at your reflection in a beautiful mirror.

Begin by saying in your mind, "I am sorry." Repeat it as many times as you'd like. Notice how your body feels when you "say" it.

Next, add, "Please forgive me." As with the previous phrase, repeat it as many times as you'd like.

Take a moment to tune into your breath again and reground yourself if you need to.

Next, in your mind, say, "I love you." Repeat it as many times as it feels comfortable. Notice how your body responds to this phrase.

Finally, "Thank you." Just as you did with the previous phrases, repeat it as many times as you would like.

✳ *How do you heal yourself with Ho'opnopono Three Steps:*

✳ *By recognizing whatever comes into your creation, the outcome of bad memories buried in your mind.*

✳ *By regretting whatever errors of body, speech and mind caused by bad memories.*

✳ *By requesting Devine Intelligence within yourself to release those memories, to set you free, then of course, say thank-you.*

Dr. Joe Vitale

Awareness on Feelings Got a Problem?

I'm Sorry that some aspect of my being or my programming or my ancestry triggered this judgment of me.

I'm sorry that I overacted and forgot my peace.

I'm sorry that my unconscious programming caused this person to judge me harshly.

Please forgive me for judging you as being insensitive.

Please forgive my ancestors for whatever they did or thought that brought that belief system into your being today.

Please forgive me for being oblivious to my inner thoughts.

Please forgive me for not being aware of my own programming, of my own beliefs of my negativity, of my past memories.

Please forgive me and I'm sorry for not being alert in a conscious, responsible way to how I've helped create this problem I'm perceiving.

Thank you for bringing this belief and data to my awareness.

Thank you for hearing my plea to erase this data from my mind, and from all minds.

Thank you for helping me to appreciate my acquaintance giving me this opportunity to clean and clear and break free.

Thank you for reminding me of love under all the darkness.

I love you,

I love my acquaintances,

I love myself,

I love my ancestors,

I love the Divine for erasing all inner limitations and data so I can be here now to experience the miracle of this moment and the miracle of love.

I love you, I love you, I love you

You have to remember it's not about the other person. It's about yourself and what you're really doing is forgiving yourself.

Dr. Joe Vitale &

Dr. Ihaleakala Hew Len, PhD

Quotes from Zero Limits

"The entire point of modern-day Ho'oponopono

is to delete the data in yourself.

Complete responsibility means accepting it all— even the people who enter your life and their problems, because their problems are your problems. They are in your life, and if you take full responsibility for your life, then you have to take full responsibility for what they are experiencing, too.

• There's nothing to do but clean

• The more you clean, the more you can receive inspiration from the Divine.

• There's either memory or inspiration, and usually it's memory (data).

• The only think to clean is what you feel inside.

• The only goal is freedom - to be at Zero."

Dr. Ihaleakala Hew Len, PhD

"If you have ever noticed if there is a problem, you are always there"!

No one can make you mad or upset; you do that inside yourself from what you perceive outside yourself.

First step is to notice you don't feel good.

Start to Clean on the Feeling - It's not about cleaning the other person, thought, situation, or anything out there. The problem is inside of you.

I'm the one aware of a problem

I'm the one who has to clean it

Say the Mantra ("I Love you, Please forgive me, I'm Sorry, Thank you") nonstop in your mind while feeling the problem as YOU perceive it. Say them to the Divine in any order.

Let go until prompted to take inspired action. Dr. Hew Len says "clean on a decision three times. If the answer is the same after those cleanings, he takes action on it. This Means that if I get and impulse to do something to resolve the perceived problem, you might clean on it three times before you actually take any action. This is a way to ensure the action is coming from inspiration and not memory.

And finally........

Ho'oponopono is a method of creating perfect order and balance to heal a situation.

Family healing and resolution I am sorry, please forgive me for anything in me that may be contributing to my experience of this problem with my family. I am cleaning with my experience of _____.

I am sorry, please forgive me for anything in me that is not Love.

I am sorry, please forgive me for anything in me that may be contributing to my experience and thoughts of being stuck.

I am cleaning with my ideas and assumptions of what it means to do "non-stop" cleaning. I am cleaning with self-judgments.

I am cleaning with thoughts that I have so much to do within myself that I do not want to do anything else.

I am sorry that I perceive it as being stuck.

I am sorry for thoughts that "cleaning self" is disconnected to my experience of being inspired.

I appreciate everyone's cleaning! I'm grateful for this opportunity to free myself through Ho'oponopono!

Peace Begins with Me

Peace Of I

I'm Sorry!

Please forgive me!

Thank You!

Printed in Great Britain
by Amazon